This Christmas Coloring Book
Belongs To:

____

____

Date: ______ / ___ / ___

Write and Draw to Express Yourself

Date:

Date: _____/_____/_____

Write and Draw to Express Yourself

Date: _______ / ___ / ___

Date: ___/___/___

Write and Draw to Express Yourself

Date: / /

Write and Draw to Express Yourself

Date: _______/____/____

Date: ___ / ___ / ___

Write and Draw to Express Yourself

Date: ___/___/___

Date: _____ / _____ / _____

Write and Draw to Express Yourself

Date: ___/___/___

Write and Draw to Express Yourself

Date: ___ / ___ / ___

Date: ___/___/___

Write and Draw to Express Yourself

Date:
xmas

Write and Draw to Express Yourself

Write and Draw to Express Yourself

Date:

Write and Draw to Express Yourself

Date: ___ / ___ / ___

Date: ___/___/___

Date: ___ / ___ / ___

Christmas
Time

Date: _____ / ____ / ______

Write and Draw to Express Yourself

Date: ___ / ___ / ___

Write and Draw to Express Yourself

Date: _______ / ____ / _______

Write and Draw to Express Yourself

Date: ___ / ___ / ___

Date: _____ / ___ / ___

Write and Draw to Express Yourself

Date:

Merry Christmas

Date: _______/____/____

Write and Draw to Express Yourself

Date: ___/___/___

Write and Draw to Express Yourself

Date: _____ / ___ / _______

Write and Draw to Express Yourself

Date: _____ / ___ / ___

Write and Draw to Express Yourself

Date:

Write and Draw to Express Yourself

Date: ___/___/___

Write and Draw to Express Yourself

Date: _____ / ___ / _____

Write and Draw to Express Yourself

Date: ___/___/___

Write and Draw to Express Yourself

Date: ___ / ___ / ___

Write and Draw to Express Yourself

The
Magic of
Christmas

Write and Draw to Express Yourself

Write and Draw to Express Yourself

Date: ___ / ___ / ___

Write and Draw to Express Yourself

Write and Draw to Express Yourself

Date: _____ / _____ / _____

Write and Draw to Express Yourself

Date: ___/___/___

Write and Draw to Express Yourself

Date: / /

Write and Draw to Express Yourself

Date:

Write and Draw to Express Yourself

Write and Draw to Express Yourself

Write and Draw to Express Yourself

peace
&
joy

Write and Draw to Express Yourself

Date:

Write and Draw to Express Yourself

Date: / /

Date: _____/_____/_____

Write and Draw to Express Yourself

Date: ___ / ___ / ___

Write and Draw to Express Yourself

Date: _____ / _____ / _____

Write and Draw to Express Yourself

Date: /   /

Date: _____ / _____ / _____

Write and Draw to Express Yourself

Date: _______/_____/_____

Write and Draw to Express Yourself

Date: ___ / ___ / ______

Date: _____ / ____ / ________

Write and Draw to Express Yourself

Write and Draw to Express Yourself

Date: ___/___/___